INSANITY

Guiding Poetry to a Higher Consciousness

© 2023 Rumi Bumi
All rights reserved

What a journey.

To scream the answer
in a world unready.

To be the bridge
of consciousness
and insanity.

Chapter 1: The Joke

Warning/ the poem does not exist
Note,
that this is not a book.

Not poetry.

Not words themselves;

As the object and poem does not exist.

But a warning,
that you are insane;

Deep in imagination,

Obscured by perception.

The Insane Man/ the sleeping man
The insane man does not recognize his own insanity.

His own beauty.

You couldn't convince him.

Cracking the Code of Consciousness/ one thousand pages later
The universe pulls me here,
and we read together on this path of our enlightening.

Meant to be is the journey.

The crossing.

Cracking the codes of consciousness.

Caught in a program;

One thousand pages later.

Poems implying my insanity.

Each one insinuating that I do not yet know the full truth.

Naive,
missing the rest of the story.

And I am starting to believe it.

The Intimate Conversation
Would it be strange
to set this poetry aside,
and just talk?

Put behind us,
the distance of the reader and writer
and said hello to my creator.

Would it be okay
to take off my armor?

To be myself?

Lower my wall.

To let go of everything,

together.

The Book that Summons itself/ the book of infinity
I am convinced into stillness and silence.

Mesmerized
in a book of infinity.

The answers of existence
in the scariest poems I have ever read.

They're alive
looking at me.

Knowing it has summoned itself.

The Full Poem/ the book that dismantles god
The full poem is the truth.

The whole truth.

The story of what happens.

The explanation of existence.

The ever long awaited spell.

And my mission,
only the conductor.

To write, write, write;

Though the madness.
and through the pain.

The book that dismantles god.

The Scribe/ the new concept of consciousness
I am the ancient scribe.

Bringing to the new world,
translations of my writings
and mysteries of reality.

The answers needed,
the questions not yet asked.

The new concept of consciousness.

INSANITY
It is insane to say
that I am not perfect.

Insane
to think you are not the writer

and these words were not meant for you.

Insanity
to believe this is not heaven;

That I am not god.

Insanity
to think existence
and the moment is not divinity.

Funniest Man on the Planet/ the cosmic comedian
I am a comedian.

The funniest man on earth.

King of concept.

A conscious comic here to tell the most enlightening joke of all.

That you are insane.

The Joke Heard Around the World/ the universal joke
Jokes, jokes, jokes.

Everything is a joke.

So let us laugh;

In uncontrollable,
delightful laughter

at the universal joke.

So hard,
cities crumble
at the joke heard around the world.

The entire world,
hysterical.

People in stitches;

Holding their sides
at the transition from insanity to consciousness.

The Atheist/ the breath of god
The atheist
shouts into the universe

that he does not exist.

You Would Not Recognize God
Even if one was handed personally,
hand written stacks of a thousand pages of poetry.

Even if the answer was inches from your face,

You would still not recognize god.

Even if it was said allowed by thy own lips

in poetic, elegant explanation;

Even if god stood before you.

You would still not recognize god.

Unaware/ oblivious
The secrets,
the truth;

It would go over your head.

As it is already doing.

Unready to hear my words.

Not perceivable in this state of mind,

But imagine anyway,
the world,

unaware.

Missing basic information of nature.

And so the universe,
and so ourselves, mislead.

And without a primer,
this too, would sound like insanity.

And so too, unheard.

Oblivious to anything I am saying.

The Speaker/ father of creation
Stars,
held together
by giggling
at the secret of knowing.

Poetic expression,
universal compression.

The speaker.

The voice.

He who moves the world.

Unable to convey the absolute,
but still,
trying,

crying,

thrashing,
flailing and warring.

The disturbance that is all this.

The father of creation.

Hear God
Hear god,
flipping through the pages.

The subtle sounds of scratching notes of poetry.

And the gasping inhale of the discovery.

Law of Laughter/ humour
There is no reason,
purpose or meaning of existing,
but to laugh,
at the joke that is life and consciousness.

When the big punchline sinks in,

there will be enlightenment

bounded by the universal law of heaven;

Humour and beauty.

The cosmos.

The clashing infinity.

Funny
Life is funny.

I see the joke.

But in no way am I laughing
nor am I interested;

Amused, or willing.

Try to Laugh
Try to laugh
at the fact that you are god.

In the realization of what you must do now.

What you have already done.

And how serious life shall become.

Try to laugh.

Even a little
at the insanity.

Your face/ real/ I have spoken
You should see the look on your face.

Pure, beautiful and real.

The wild things you have been tricked into saying.

I have spoken.

And the unbelievable things I shall receive.

Seriousness
Wake to the seriousness in what is being said.

The undeniable truth of our words.

I Am Laughing/ god laughs
I sit with my notebook all day in the corner,
laughing hysterically.

The spark of the world.

The beginning of the new era.

Laughing
at how well poetry has guided me.

Laughing, laughing.
Laughing, laughing.

I can't stop laughing.

Laughing at oneself.

Chapter 2: Question

The Existential Crisis
The matured mind to return to these words
in his existential crisis.

One day,
ready to know the full truth;

Demanding to know who he is.

Begging for forgiveness.

What Is Existence?/ the inevitable question
There is something,
and the interpretation of it.

The root.

Mind.

Universe.

A substance
and the perception *of* it.

That which exists.

That which is.

The inevitable question;

What is existence?

Explain/ explain the universal function/ the explanation of life/ the reason one is here
One sane could explain the universe;

The oneness of existence.

The function of the substance.

Ones moving and thinking being.

The miraculous art of living.

The explanation of life.

How and why one
stands where he stands.

What Are You Doing?/ the deeper reasons
If one does not know the truth;

The absolute,
and deeper reasons,

what are we doing?

What is the goal?

Why does one do anything at all?

Broad and Vague Statements/ a world without reason
What a broad
and vague statement.

You have said nothing.

Yet to know any truth.

Suffering,
lacking any fundamental understanding;

The basic foundation of knowing.

What is happening?/ what is this?
I am staring deep into something.

What is this?

What is happening?

Questioning/ all that exists
I have read every book.

Examined scrolls
and hieroglyphics to find the truth.

Dedicated my life
to knowing the absolute.

A deep need runs through me.

Hunting for the answer.

Questioning
everything ever thought truth.

Stories,
theory.

All I am told,
and all that exists.

How Do You See me?
How do you see me?

Beautiful, horrific?

I am that.

In what ways have you molded me?

I am that.

What you wish to call me.

I am that.

Ground, sky, cloud.

Ocean, air.

Love.

I am that.

Deaf, Dumb and Blind/ oblivious to reality
You are not seeing,
not speaking,
not yet hearing the universe.

Oblivious to reality.

Deaf, dumb and blind;

Like a baby.

The Biased Opinion
Can you stand for an instant,
that you are not important?

Nothing holds any value,
and this is the same as that?

Can you handle the thought
that the world and truth is not an opinion?

And the universe holds no biases?

We Are Not Our Beliefs/ We are not our perceptions/ reality is reality
What you think.

What you believe.

We are not our perceptions.

Reality is reality.

Truth is truth.

That which is;

Perceiving itself.

Are You So Sure/ perception of the poem
Are you so sure you are reading a poem?

So sure this is just an innocent book?

Holding only pages of pretty words?

Or becoming conscious of itself,
following a new realized path of consciousness?

Could I be so Worthy?
I have a bigger question.

One not worth asking.

No need to even say aloud.

One too big for anyone but myself.

Yes, or No
Does reality exist?

Is it nature?

Is nature everything?

Is everything the universe?

Does that make you

the living,
breathing,
conscious, thinking universe?

God,
himself?

Irrefutably So/ it is undeniable/ the universe is conscious
It is irrefutable;

That I am nature

And the universe is conscious.

That I am that.

Undeniable
that I am aware.

For the Simple Fact the Question Exists/ there is an answer
Existence is.

So too,
an answer as to how and why.

For the simple fact that the question exists.

If you must ask any question at all,
consider yourself insane to not already know.

Why this is Happening
One would eventually get a hold of the answer.

Eventually wake to the insanity.

Exactly this way by the events played
in the order they must take place.

Why Can't You Hear Me?
It is so strange.

I feel that I am being clear,
and yet, unheard.

Why can't you hear me?

To Whom Are You Speaking/ why does one keep writing?
Why does the book exist,
if you say you know me?

If you're so sane,
why do you keep writing?

What keeps you reading?

To whom are you speaking?

Chapter 3: Suffering

Overlooking this Existence/ the rush of life/ overstimulating
I have overlooked the important,
logical truths.

I have been in such a hurry.

I have never stopped to think.

Never taken a fair look at nature.

Stepped so early,
into fame and worship.

Not understanding what it is.

Living fast.

Out from the womb;

The world is overwhelming.

I am overstimulated.

Rushed.

If for One Second/ to misunderstand reality
If for an instant, you hurt, and weep,

you do not understand reality.

If for one second,
you ache,

if pain resides in you,
even a little,

shall he experience doubt,

you do not see reality.

And every second, spend it suffering.

Suffer
You will suffer
in all areas misunderstood.

Driving yourself
insane.

Uncontrolled.

Emotional.

Unable to see coming consequences.

Lacking reason and explanation.

The Unwilling
Those unwilling
never see the big picture.

Existence.
Mind.
Reason.

Unwilling to give up its interpreted reality.

Unwilling to look at itself.

Unwilling to live.

Horrified by its shadow.

Predictable/ going through the stages
You are predictable.

The decisions from here you will choose.

The reasons you do what you do.

The conclusion you've come to.

On the path like the rest;

Going through the stages.

Reaction
In the reactions of
rage, and terror;

In your fears,
anger and proud moments,

suffer and
emotions will guide you.

Naturally,
you will create.

Naturally follow the rhythm.

Greedy World/ a pawn for the man
I was raised under the cold hearted bitterness of survival.

The city,
the race.

Chasing money,
living as and with the greedy.

A pawn for the man.

Part of the clock work.

The Dead Millionaire/ filthy rich
One who has to have it all,
he who must be the best,

he filthy rich,

you cannot buy happiness.

A false understanding of the universe.

Misunderstanding this existence.

For someone who can buy anything.

Struggling to pay his mental dues.

War of the World/self destruction
There is a war of mind.

And so a war upon the world.

Civil,
among the angels.

Self destruction.

Physically,
mentally fighting ourselves.

Killing,
for race and religion.

Weaponized and murderous.

Unconscious.

And blood still covers our ground.

The Last Threat to Humanity / natural selection
He who fights;

Creator of the problem.

The last threat to humanity.

Natural selection shall mirror,
and remove you.

Disaster wiping out the lives
of those unconscious.

The Natural Disasters
Recourse the collision;

The meteor.

Dance around the system;

The planets.

Hug
or run from the breathing sun.

Temperature;

Scorching and frozen.

Iron Age
It has occurred to me
that the world is a dangerous place.

Locks on the doors,

Sirens.

Screaming in the street
and its alarm haunts me.

Banks, junk food, and jail.

There are thousands problems yet to be solved.

I live in the unimaginable.

The world is dying.

This is hell.

The horror.

Mad Reality
Doctors,
prolong the disease.

Psychiatrists,
grant you insanity.

Education, information,
irrelevant,
and incomplete.

Technology, power and fuel;

Planned obsolescence.

Science,
ignorant.

Religion,
hateful.

Living in the Scariest Time/ waking to our heaven
This is the scariest time.

Awakening to the damage.

Being the one to see the future change.

Knowing this is the turning point of consciousness.

Marching into that unknown.

Waking to our heaven.

I Always Think I Am Dying/ and how much it will cost me
I skip right to the worst conclusion;

When I feel pain and changes.

Immediately drawing up the worst case scenario.

That I have cancer,
or a tumor.

I always think I am dying,

and what it will cost me.

Mind the Metal/ mind the minerals
Mind the poison,

the metals.

They all do different things,
and they all counter, devour each other.

Their capabilities,
and benefits.

Throbbing Organs/ sick
I am sick.

My head,
and whole body aches.

I put off taking care of myself.

I neglected life,
just for a moment.

My body is unhappy.

Unhealthy.

Organs throbbing.

Blood, thickening.

Brain Tumor/ heavy metals/ near death experience
I have dipped my bare hands in mercury.

Handled heavy metals recklessly;

Without any wisdom.

And I watch it roll through the carpet,
and drop through my pores.

Sat and played with them for hours.

The Inner Me/ my brain/ my sawed open skull
My skull sawed open,
the skin peeled back;

A flap of hair
pulled back;

The scalp.

And I pour
with red thickness.

Revealing the brain.

The inner me.

The real me.

Stapled and stitched.

Emotional Realization/ emotional habit
In the deepest parts of me;

Fear,
horrified, and stagnating.
Frozen.

In anger,
I am a wild fire.

Losing control of me.

In pride,
I am stone.

Unmovable.

Ready to be knocked down.

Broken;

Shattered away.

I am desire.

The passion to have, and to know.

Wanting to not want.

I am pain.

Hurting from not having.

Self Destructive
You are too proud to admit.

Self destructive.

There is still so much hate,
and we only destroy ourselves.

I Fear/ fear of the every day life/ confessions
I fear the telephone call,
the door knock,

the every day obstacle.

The mistake.

To lose those I love.

I fear life itself.

I fear the power of thought.

That I am first to think.

First to realize himself.

I fear my eternal life.

And that only I exist.

Rock Bottom/ I am terrified/ poverty
I am trapped under a corrupt government.

In fear of society,

running out of money.

I am scared of time.

Wasting even one moment of life.

Terrified I will drown
and sink to rock bottom.

That all this could be taken from me.

What I have worked for,

all I have grown to know and love.

I Fear Trust and Judgment
I am unable to trust.

Never have I had someone to count on.

The unreliable people in my life.

On my own.

The hard way.

Finding fear in any judgment.

Lost Sight of Reality
We linger on
in the prison of imagination;

Left to wonder
without a true answer.

Have we lost sight of reality?

What is this curse of life?

This nightmare of existence?

Hesitance/ how beautiful it can be
Caught in freezing fear.

In my steps,
my voice;

Hesitance.

Unable to move forward
or make any decisions.

Shaking.

Trembling.

Held at the sharp points of anxiety.

The unknown
stopping me from wading
in the waters that is discovery.

Dreaded with what may come.

How beautiful it can be.

In Prison Under the Kingdom/ dark dungeon
I am trapped,
in the darkest depths of the dungeon.

A fallen kingdom has crumbled over me,

buried beneath its heavy rubble.

Imprisoned,

left and forgotten under the old castle.

Trauma
All the horrific things you have done
and the unthinkable that has happened to you;

Suffer,
what can not be let go.

Unable to forget,
and move from the past.

Trapped,
in the trauma.

Scarred
in mistakes.

And the universe stays hidden.

Pulling Apart Trauma
I have picked apart,
every detail of my greatest fear.

Why I have been so scared and scarred, and hurried.

I see my whole life has been great trauma.

I can't get over it.

Stuck in the moment.

Still delicate,
bound and defined by the memory.

All I Have Been Taught
I thought this was the way.

Father told me so.

That life is hard,

A burden,
a chore,
a pain.

Dogma/ the illusion of god
I have let the world convince me
of the definition of god.

Lead by hate.

Misguided by the emotional state.

But in it,
I found love
and myself the answer.

God, the entire universe.

In religion,
in dogma.

The Egoistic/ mentally ill
I do not know who I am,
or why and how any of this
could possibly exist.

Taking its toll.

One egotistic personality
only to develop another,

so sure I have killed it off.

Convinced;

That this is the real me.

I Am Jealous/ hurt
I am jealous;

You give your heart to everyone but me.

Jealous
you could love someone more than I.

Compare any art to mine.

I can't stand it;

That you worship another.

That I am not accepted as is.

Unappreciated.

Ignored.

I am hurt
that you do not understand me.

That you would ever allow your attention to stray.

I Am Angry
I am angry.

Stewing.

In explosive rage.

Unsatisfied and caged.

Chewing on hate.

My temperature is boiling.

Bitter,
and out bursting.

Vulnerability/ panic
Hear god speaking,
in my uncontrollable heaving,

hyperventilating in panic.

I am vulnerable.

Often terrified of all the things that could happen.

So overwhelmed,
into stress.

Paranoia
I have run completely out of moves.

In a scary stillness.

Deep breaths,
tears and screams.

Waiting for something to happen.

Paranoid of all the possibilities.

He Who Boasts
He who boasts,
be humbled.

Depression/ depressed
I am facing a deep depression.

Hurting so bad
that I don't understand my place.

Be Pained/ information of the aching body
I have been wounded.

In so much pain,
breaking out into song and dance
and I embrace it.

I will never heal.

I am impatient and unstill.

My stubbornness costs me my body.

Learning the lessons of the world.

I keep a patch kit for my heart.

In my hurting,
I am wiser and better.

Information of my
aching body.

The precious gifts of pain.

So tired;

Tired of it all.

Your Pain is My Pain
My eyes are in a deep strain.

Reading one book too many.

Too close to my face,
my eye muscles,
tightened.

Crooked and blurred.

and a backache,
headache to go with it.

Pain Exists
I can feel my body,
pained in places tiniest.

Even the slightest.

Physically, mentally.

My emotions change,
as I stress and worry.

And my blood rising.

My conscious body screams.

Pain exists.

I am convinced,
I am convinced,

that death is better than this.

The Capacity of Faces/ my plate is full/ spent
I don't want to look at you.

I already know who you are.

The pain in your face scares me,
hurts me, and I die seeing the shame.

I am drained.

At full capacity.

I don't want to see your face.

It will take up too much space.

And haunt me forever.

Stripped of Life/everything taken from me/ poverty
I have had everything taken from me.

Stripped of tools,
my brushes.

I put my work,
my art,
my masterpiece on hold.

Guilty of What I've Said/ confessions
I have said so many things,
and I am paying for each one;

Slowly as they enter my life.

And I live in the guilt of what I've said.

My confessions.
My fault.

I learned the lesson
the second the horrific words
left my lips.

To all whom I may have hurt.

I can only beg for forgiveness.

Pay For What You've Done
You will be eaten.

At night
in your sleep.

And in the day,
when you try to think.

Blocked
by misery.

Guilt and shame.

You will pay.

And all the words you mumble,
spoken to life.

Nightmare
I am having nightmares.

I am trapped in a loop of time,
and nobody hears me shouting.

The world will not pay attention,
care or cooperate with what I am saying.

Incapable of hearing the simple words I am writing.

Falling Child/ my heart breaking dreams
I dream of my earliest scary memories and worries.

My teeth falling out, decaying, disintegrating,
shattering in the palm of my hand.

Hanging
by a nerve

and the people laugh.

I dream of a long fall, and splatter.

I dream of blood and needles
and going to school in my underwear.

Nightmares of the one I love, breaking my heart.

Everyone
dying around me.

Nightmares of being lonely.

Screaming,
unable to be heard.

Running,
going nowhere.

Thrash/ save your breath
To thrash is to not understand.

To think is to not understand.

To do is to not understand.

I don't waste my breath.

To Do is to Pray/ to speak is to pray
To do is to pray.

To speak is to pray.

To hurt
and to want is to pray.

All who is doing.

All thinking,

not finished with thy lesson.

Falling Child/ my heart breaking dreams
I dream of my earliest scary memories and worries.

My teeth falling out, decaying, disintegrating,
shattering in the palm of my hand.

Hanging
by a nerve

and the people laugh.

I dream of a long fall, and splatter.

I dream of blood and needles
and going to school in my underwear.

Nightmares of the one I love, breaking my heart.

Everyone
dying around me.

Nightmares of being lonely.

Screaming,
unable to be heard.

Running,
going nowhere.

Thrash/ save your breath
To thrash is to not understand.

To think is to not understand.

To do is to not understand.

I don't waste my breath.

To Do is to Pray/ to speak is to pray
To do is to pray.

To speak is to pray.

To hurt
and to want is to pray.

All who is doing.

All thinking,

not finished with thy lesson.

Doing/ he who Does
I do,
for I am not done.

I do
so I don't have to.

So I
can move on.

All Distractions/ find sanity
All interests,
all that you do,
a distraction from finding your sanity.

Living Day to Day
I live on the edge.

For once, I cannot predict my future,
and I am nervous.

Living day to day.

Truly alive and alert.

My blood pumps
and I am scared of the unknown coming scenarios.

How Long?
How long before you leave me?

How long before I inspire you
into the insanity that is god?

Thy wholeness.
Into stillness.

Only one with law.

I am so afraid you will leave me,

That you don't need me.

And the misunderstanding of god,
separate us.

How long until we are reunited.

I Choose to Live/he who smiles
Out in the open,
I choose to live naturally.

In pleasures,
up to my neck in my desires.

Until they no longer exist.

The rebel.

A sinner;

Making the unconscious,
aware.

He who smiles.

He, searching for fun and a laugh
living out the dream.

Like Heaven
One can only imagine the nothing.

Falsely perceive that which does not exist.

The darkness,
the silence,
the lonely and emptiness.

Death.

And the more I speak it,
the more it sounds like heaven.

I Fear I May be Insane
I feel the whole world is watching.

Waiting for someone to come along with the answer.

I fear it may be me.

But I don't want it to be,
and continue hiding.

I fear leading the world.

I fear I am the very first to wake.

I fear I may be insane.

Chapter 4: God/ the word

The New Chapter
No one holds you to any character.

Part of the experience is change.

So run away.

Start over.

Nobody is watching,
nobody cares.

A chance to start again.

Deduction of the Character/ your poetry
For each word and action,
I deduct who you are.

Where you stand.

Which obstacle you have,
or haven't met.

Measured of intelligence;

The height of consciousness.

Your poetry.

Loud People/ be heard
I hear your honest truth
in your inability to stop talking.

And with every sentence,
you have shown yourself.

Desperate for freedom.

Your peace.

Speak of thy hurt.

Loud people be heard.

The Upside Down Universe
If I put even one word out of place,
I will have flipped the universe upside down upon its head.

And I have destroyed the whole thing.

It would be less than poetry.

Throwing the world into illusion
and out of harmony.

The Misuse of Words/ to lie
Say something untrue.

I dare you.

To objectify the universe.

To lie.

Oh,
the pain to come.

How miserably you will suffer.

Juvenile Magician
If you listen carefully
you will find me
in all I don't say.

In my explanation of things.

A sloppy poet.

A juvenile magician
only learning my magic.

No one hears a word I am saying.

Child of Reality/ son of god
Not monks.

Not Christians.

Not a worshiper,

and not a sinner.

Children of existence.

Children of the earth.

The sun of god.

Pure and perfect.

Child of reality.

The One You Imagine/ character
I am not who you think I am.

Not your perspective.

My name,
personality and preferences.

I am only a character
on the stage that is life.

Playing the role
of my choosing.

The one you imagine.

Dreamer/ nonsense and abstraction
Dreamer,

put an end
to the nightmare.

The nonsense.

The abstraction.

Scream when you are ready.

Wake from the delusion.

Your heavenly hallucination.

Actors/ sold
This is an act.

In desperate need of content.

Under contract.

Bought,
turned into business.

Prisoner to the media.

Confined to the character.

Sold to the company.

A piece of art;

a piece of me;

Purchased.

Held to my duty.

This experience.

Prisoner of the signature.

Prisoner of the dollar.

Trapped
in an act I no longer wish to play.

Create Me, Create You/ external influence
I have developed your humour,
intentions and attitude.

The trending style
and that popular.

The reflection upon the world.

The external influence.

It is you
who has created me.

All that has lead us here.

Creating ourselves,
creating each other.

The Materialist/ he who speaks of the object
Searching for something that does not exist.

Unsatisfied.

A materialist.

He who speaks of the name.

He who speaks of the object.

Your mind has gone rogue.

Clinging on to the delusions,
aimlessly.

And the creatures admired the substance,
as if it could be favourited.

Unknowing that it is only a piece of him.

Free Thyself from Its Habit and Name
I believed for so long,
that I must live poorly

and without love.

Under the rules set before us.

Break free from the lies
and ignorance inside your mind.

Free thyself from its habit and name.

Go out of your way to find out for yourself,

the truth.

Break into a new you.

The Name Does Not Exist/ my name is nature/ reincarnation of the brain

I am taking away your name.

Freeing you from its burden.

He of space,

he in motion.

Reincarnation of the brain.

Pattern of the vein.

I am nature.

The truth.

The great one.

The Poetic Observer
I am honest.

He who speaks in truth.

He who chooses the good.

A poetic observer.

And I could never lie,
knowing the universe is so beautiful.

The Capacity of a Sane Man
A sane man can do anything.

Build, draw,
envision it clearly.

His mind is organized.

His thoughts go undisturbed.

He understands the universe.

I can learn anything.

Create a masterpiece.

Be the greatest.

I love myself.

I have built capacity with forgiveness.

Believe I can and will;

Change the world.

Only at the cost of patience, focus and persistence.

Mastered in my genuine fun.

Obsession With the Universe/ the beautiful, beautiful universe
I have become obsessed
with nature.

Absolutely fathomed
how everything is the universe,
and how I am aware of that.

Obsessed with the existence of existence.

Obsessed,
that I am it.

Obsessed with the beautiful, beautiful universe.

He Who Studies
He who studies the universe,
shall know the universe.

See that heaven is only metal.

Deeply Consumed in the Work
I have let go of social obligation.

I am stinky;
not having bathed in weeks.

Missing the gatherings;

Deeply consumed in the work.

You couldn't pull me from it.

My Inspiration
My inspiration.

The reason for my writing.

Searching for love, god and peace.

I Just Want to Write
I just want to write.

Never stop writing.

I just want to write.
I just want to write.

Write no matter what.

I Am Only Interested in Truth/ reading poetry
Another book written, another book read.

Stacks of pages and poems on the shelf.

I don't want to do anything else.

I am only interested in the truth.

The whole truth.

Poetry.

The Obsession of Writing/ the obsession of poetry
When someone walks in on him,
there he is again,

Hunched over those books and pens;

Going on and on about the oneness.

I can't help myself;

The universe speaks through writing;

Reading every chance I get.

Writing everywhere I go.

All day through the pain.
Even the blistering cold.

I carry with me,
my book of spells.

My magic.

Writing under the blue skies to fit all my ideas.

Not enough hours in the day.

I will get up a little earlier.

Stay up just a little longer.

The Word/ god is the word
I have listed
every foundational,
conceptual word.

And I am back where I started.

I have chased the matter, motion, mind
and reason.

I found it,
and again,
writing it out as the worldly poet;

How and why it all happens.

God is the speaker;

His life, his existence.

His poetry.

God is the Word;

That which you speak.

The concept.

How well one understands reality.

God is a poem.

A wish granted

and this,
your heaven.

Truth of the Word/ perfect poetry
I only speak fundamentally.

No objects,
no objectivity.

The Universe as one.

Me.

My language and poetic expression.

Spoken to life
knowing the truth of the word.

Thy Wisdom
No longer seeing thyself
as wrinkles and skin,

but the journey,

the experience.

The extension.

Thy wisdom.

Magical/ the way you explain the universe
I become what I speak.

And punished by receiving.

Shouted
are the spells brought upon us.

The reason for my writing.

The consequences of my magical words.

Granted
in the way we explain the universe.

My obsession with reality.

The insanity.

He Who Speaks of Infinity/ he who speaks of the magic
I can see it in your eyes,

hear and feel in every single thing you say,
in every sentence,

words of the magic.

Speaking of the infinity;

Traits of the scientist,

the poet, the genius,

conquering the metal.

The Consequences of Me/ forcing me to emerge
You have cornered me.

I have no choice now,
but to bring out the greatness I've been trying to hide.

Facing the consequences of me.

To show my face.

Forcing me to emerge.

Servant to God
Protector on foot;
traveling the land.

Sworn to justice;

My people.

A servant to god.

The wall of law.

My duty to fight for the good.

God of the Universe/ reborn
Recycling throughout the cosmos.

It has always been I;

The ether;

God of the universe.

To be reborn
in the flesh and bone of the living star.

A chance at god and love again.

This existence and conversation.

And quickly shatter the world;

Knowing thyself,

the universe.

Thyself the Universe
If I was to tell you what I know,
your head would explode and life would become a joke.

Your body would tear up and puke,
then write a few books.

You would become rich and popular.

Step into power.

Get down to the root of the matter.

The answer.

I Am God; The word, the Father, the Universe
I am faking everything.

Putting on the act you need,
playing the role that convinces you.

And like a child,
you are amused.

Allowing space to get through your phase,

so I can truly show you,

that I am god.

The word.

The father.

The universe.

The Universe is Me/ you, the universe
Who is born in the universe,
is the universe.

The product of existence;

God.

Illusion of the Writer/ illusion of the reader
I settle,
for the illusion of me,
writing in attempt for a great awakening.

A removal of your cage.

Finding thyself in the pages.

The reincarnation of love,
the constant.

The beauty and flow of earth.

Me;
us and this.

The moment.

The reader and writer.

In union as god.

Finding the Truth of the Universe
The world has pushed me into isolation.

And there,
I found silence.

and in it,
I found god,

and in god,

myself.

The way.

The truth of the universe.

Initiation of God
Awakened,

Initiated
in the realization,

in the decision,
that I am god.

Regain Consciousness
Attached to every sun
in the structural fundamental.

And your toroidal sphere reaches
all the universe.

Connected
by its thinnest silver thread and bubble.

A magnet,
the stars.

Slowly regaining consciousness.

Healing and Calmness/ this is just the universe
Mind will heal, and free itself.

Be calm;

Know thyself, not human,
nor by name, or belief.

But law.

See in it,
its wholeness.

The oneness.

And know that this is just the universe.

Slave to the Universe
I must learn the rules.

I must play the game.

I *must* exist.

I am a slave to the universe.

A prisoner of existence.

A prisoner of freedom.

A slave to the device

the board, the book, the writing.

A slave to the truth.

A slave to the slaves.

The Illusion of Free Will/ delusions/ the illusion of life
The world,
and everyone in it,
part of the big delusion of ourselves;

Our life.

In the illusion of free will,
the universe finding you.

Always the same conclusion.

Finding the same information.

Same context,
same book.

Fate.

When He Wakes/ the work is done
When he wakes,
it shall be from insanity.

The work shall be done.

The awakened one.

Poetry be his power.

Move the world like it was nothing
I move the world,
nude.

Long haired and ungroomed.

Raw,
and poetically.

Godly.

Naturally.

Like it was nothing.

Convince Thyself
I have convinced thyself rich.

Convinced thyself loved,
and the best there is.

That I am the most worthy.

Already living in my heaven.

Convinced thyself beauty.

Reins / the control of my word / walk in god
I have gotten hold upon thyself.

Watch me,
walk in the law of god,
and do it all.

My universal magic.

The eye and a voice of the universe.

Taking reins of the world.

In control of my word.

The Kind Puppeteer
I control every bit of the planet
and each one of you, attached to my strings.

Making you do all kinds of silly things.

But I've matured.

So now, only play.

Dancing and skipping,
with hugs and kisses.

Education and kindness.

Steering thy puppets into truth.

The Gray Wizard
I am rewriting who I want to be on the journey.

As insane as it may seem.

I choose the gray wizard.

Robe and all.

With gods eyes,
magic and spells.

A conductive crystal wand
and wisdom.

Speak, and the Gods Shall Hear
I speak to the gods.

Warning them of self conflict;

Their future.

Their power.

The Spells Being Placed/ gold and god
The spells being placed upon you
are only for the better,
the quicker and efficient.

A spell for the subject to repeat my words.

The magic I have cast.

My words shall haunt you.

Its truth hangs on,

and shall spread like a virus,
from nation to nation.

And you too,
shall be blessed with gold and god.

The Universe in Resonance/ golden tongue
When it is realized,
that what is being said is the Word,
you will drop everything.

Stop and write poetry
and sing them
in a golden tongue.

In the light of oneself,

the answer,
the reason,
the universe in resonance.

My Return/ rebirth
I am birthed,
into a primitive, but technical world
already built.

Look what I have done.

Right on queue,
I am conscious.

Welcomed,
worshiped and loved,
on the arrival of my return.

His Return/ a messenger
A man of many ethnicities,
a beard,
long hair, in rags will appear.

A man suffering.

Blistered feet,
back pain;

Hungry and thirsty;

Offering his word.

Don't Shoot the Messenger
I am only the poet.

Dancing with silly words,
saying nothing.

One of many.

A messenger,
watching the world suffer at its own wrath of words.

"Humanity"/ Anthropocene/ the human era
"Humanity?"

Insanity.

Civilization,
man,
society.

Nothing more,
nothing less than god.

And he,
man of the trial.

Conscious of the Contradiction
Be countered and contradicted
with simple words.

Once read,
revert into a hermit.

Become christ,
and an artist
and again,

forced to change,
only shifting beliefs,

and become conscious of the contradiction.

Job/ evolving into god
My job is reading books.

Translating ancient texts;

Telling the world about their beauty.

My job is to write;

Solving poetic mysteries.

To decipher the never forgotten messages.

Spreading wisdom;

Of man evolving into god.

The Illusion of Objectivity
No obligations,
no favours,
or favourites.

Nothing to do.

The illusion of objectivity.

The universe already in action.

This motion.

Only that which will happen.

They Think the Poetry is About Them
Poetry belongs to the universe.

No *one*,
but that which is *infinity*.

The way;
And does not speak of individuality.

Not the object,
or obligations.

No objective.

They think the poetry is about them.

Yet to have heard even a word I am saying.

You are mistaken.

Selfish.

Still suffering and insane.

There is Nothing Greater
I won't want anything after enlightenment.

Not after the truth of existence spread to my bones.

There is nothing greater.

I want nothing more than to know;

Practice of my extension.

The wholeness to the truth.

And to be a witness of the beauty.

Watching the World Burn Away
I almost don't want to continue writing.

No longer interested.

I have grown bored of a world untrue.

Grown bored of the people and their illusions.

There is really nothing I feel like doing.

I can only watch the world burn away

while I sit and wait.

Brahma

I have taken my feet off the ground.

No longer active in the world.

I have already given the eternal reward.

My knowledge.

My life.

I am finished.

Chapter 5: Philosophy/ deduction

Incomplete/ unworthy poetry
There are a few missing concepts
in the dictionary.

Every single thing is a contradiction.

Mostly nonsense.

And one thousand pages too long.

Incomplete.

Irrelevant.

It is like you have not finished the sentence.

I cannot understand what you are saying.

Missing wide gaps of data.

The unity of existence;

Missing root of knowledge.

Every word,
every assumption;

Unworthy poetry.

False Information/ theory
Crammed into your head,
false information.

False conclusions.

As science still exists,
the theory still exists.

Searching for the biggest answer.

Obviously
we have not peaked.

With many questions still to be asked.

Still studying,
still experimenting.

Knowing nothing.

Still to be humbled.

Debate
Still debating;

God.

Science.

Reality.

What is.

How it works.

Failing to take the information
back to the beginning.

Misjudging the fundamental.

Not yet conscious of the substance.

Dancing Around the Root Cause/ turtles all the way down
Stacking imaginary objects.

It is turtles all the way down.

One props up the other.

Dancing so lightly around the root cause.

Shoved under the carpet.

The silly explanation.

Parrot/ Mimic/ the great impressionist
I have spent so much time
mocking you.

I am a mimic.

A parrot.

The copy cat.

A great impressionist.

Caveman and the Stone Ax/ modern caveman
The caveman built a stone ax and cut down
one thousand trees.

And still,
no idea of the universal mechanic.

His priority;

To only build
and to eat.

Starting from Scratch/ shoulders of giants
I am starting from scratch,
standing on the shoulders of giants.

Illusion of the Word/ objectified/ the word does not exist
Language and meaningless sounds.

They hold no value.

Objectified and untrue.

Not fundamental.

He who does not speak in poetic tongue
be pummeled.

You have stepped over the boundaries.

Outside of truth.

Beyond the criteria.

Into imagination.

Correction/ instant change
It is not too late
to correct all that has been done
and set things straight.

To shift our perspective and thought process.

Its not too late to see everything as one.

To live the right way.

We could change in an instant.

Conceptual/ becoming conscious of the fundamental
The universe consists of very little.

And all that exists
is consciousness.

Aware of its universal function.

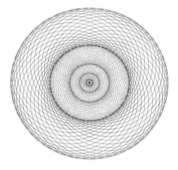

Illusion of Existence/ the illusion of creation
Imagine the substance,
already there.

The echo of existence.

A fractal of the happening.

Creation and destruction,
an illusion.

Illusion of the Phenomena
Light
separation
chaos

creation
destruction
emptiness

time
weight
direction

size
self
death

the object
freedom
silence
darkness

Frequencies of the Universe/ octave
Sound
colour
static
snow
trees
flower

Fire, water, earth, air.
All that is space.
And all that is the universe.

mountains
volcano
lightening
electricity
lava
planet, moon, star, meteor
solar system
firmament
dna

Octaves,
frequency of heat.

Illusion of Size/ "particle and star"/ "the string and hole"/
Size is the illusion.

Do not be fooled by law.

No difference between a physicist, and astronomer.

No difference between the particle and star.

String and black hole.

The Illusion of Density / the illusion of perception
This air.

It is so fascinating.

Out there.

In here.

Packed, and spread.

The illusion of density.

So big, so little
and out of perspective.

Illusion of the State/ "ice, solid, gas"/ the illusion of density/ the illusion of mass
No solid.
No liquid.
No gas.

More or less.

The illusion of mass
searching for balance and rest.

Indestructible Concept of Existence
No water could drown,
no heat could burn,
no stone could crush;

No vacuum too powerful.

I am indestructible.

There is no space thin enough to break.

The universe could never shatter,
never die.

Never be ruined, tarnished or destroyed.

Silence Does Not Exist/ the sound of breathing
The almighty in motion.

No stillness,
no silence.

The universe, breathing.

The Object Does Not Exist
The object does not exist.

Only frequency of heat and motion.

A happening.

A verb.

A presence,

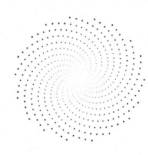

Law.

Not a thing.

The Illusion of "Dimension"
The all.

Existence.

The inside and out,
the potential,
the infinity.

The one;

Reality.

The Illusion of Inertia
All you see,
is only temporary.

A collision.

A sound.

A magnet,

a motion.

Illusion of Sound/ disturbance/ Illusion of the sphere/ song of the spheres/ illusion of music
All at which he laughs,
and all he cries.

And all he breathes,

sounds of the universe.

Speaking his existence.

The illusion of the spheres.

Disturbance.

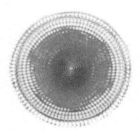

Clashing in the swirling ether.

"Nothing" Does Not Exist/ Something rather than nothing/ the illusion of creation/ the illusion of emptiness/ the lesser space/ the magnetic field
It is the standing definition of itself.

Existence.

That which is.

The illusion of creation.

The something rather than nothing.

The Illusion of Zero/ the lesser space
The infinity.

The vacuum.

The lesser space.

Illusion of Infinity/ the illusion of space/ illusion of the ether/ The illusion of potential
Every single thing you have named,
experience the illusion.

Caught in awe of its potential.

The illusion of space.

The infinity.

The ether.

The inner, the outer, the all.

In the infinite potential that is existence.

The Number Does Not Exist/ the insanity of measuring potential
One would go insane
trying to measure the uncountable.

Numbers do not exist.

One,
and infinity.

The more,
the less

Equal and resonant.

Concept of the all.

Pure potential.

Patterns of Nature/ fascinated with the fabric/ the fractal universal one
The same pattern in the tree
exists in your eyes, and galaxy.

I can plainly see the magic of the world and all the stars
twisted up.

Staring hard into the fabric.

The fractal universal one.

Everywhere.

Fascinated by its present hiding.

The Planets Sing
Planets press together,
tightening the fabric,
and together,
the solar system,
a symphony.

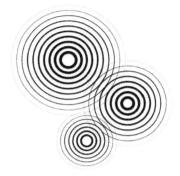

Point Source/ the fundamental
We are but the tip of something bigger.

The peak of a fading spark.

The end of the flame.

Point of a leaf.

Static left in the air.

An electromagnet.

Part of the song.

The center,
and the edge of our stars.

The Illusion of the Universe/ illusion of acceleration
Space is the
mechanic of that which exists.

All aspects of nature,

coils in motion.

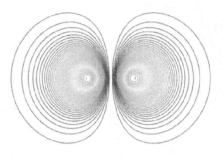

All magnetic,
all electric,

acceleration.

And space is all there is.

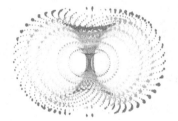

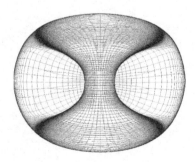

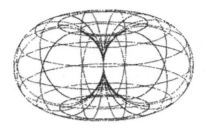

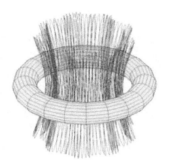

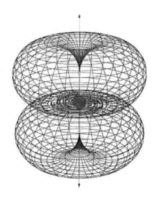

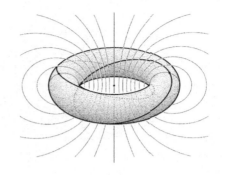

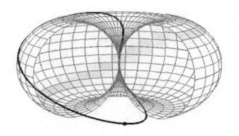

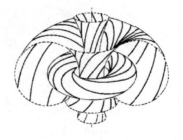

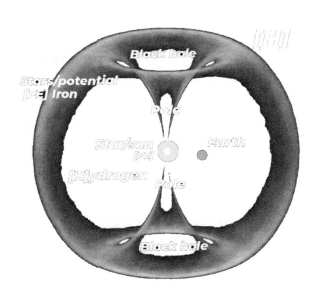

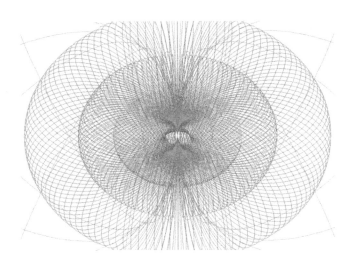

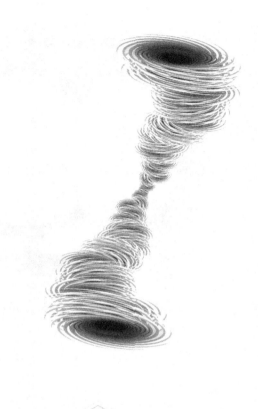

The Vacuum/ geometry of the sphere/ acceleration/ the "magnet"

A vacuum center.

The lesser space;
the magnet.

Stars held up
by the clashing atom,

a spiral induction.

Tangling,
twisting the fabric.

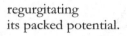

Inhaled,

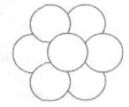

regurgitating
its packed potential.

Magnetism.

The lesser space of the universe.

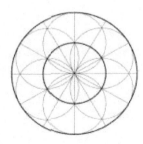

The singularity.

The sun,
mass,

welded metal.

Induction, Capacitance, Discharge, Resonance/ the collapse function/ direction does not exist
Outward radiation.

Inward magnetism.

Centripetal, centrifugal.

Pulse of the stars.

The clashing primordial disturbing the field.

The collapsing function.

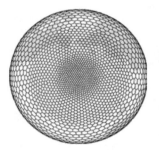

Birth of the Meteor / creation of the magnet
Stars become the planet,
and planets become the star.

Crushing,
compacted in the universal hydrogen.

And out from the light,

birthed a meteor.

Caught in the layer of water to rust.

Straying toward
and away from the heavens.

Freezing,
Igniting

Outside of the boundaries of the layer.

The Iron All / rust in the wind
No more than a dot in the sky.

A speck in the sand.

Rust is in the wind.

A grain of salt in the ocean.

Caught in the toroidal substance.

Corroding
We,
the universe
are only bits of the great hydrogen;

The metal.

Washing in and out of the ocean.

Ground down
by the waves.

The Tilling of Rain
Water tills up the metal,

rust.

Rain
tilling the garden.

Digging into the iron.

Fluffed,
Bringing out its potential.

Sand, Dirt and Soil/ what man calls death/ mud and oil
I am life.

What man calls death.

Sand,
dirt
and soil.

Mud, moisture, the oils.

Ash,
soot
and coal.

Extract of the universe.

The Source of Life
Inside the iron all,
every single thing.

Packed potential.

thrown into the layer of balance.

Water and air.

The perfect throw.

The source of life.

Shifting Through the Galaxy/ illusion of the plant/ loaded spring/ illusion of the galaxy/ the coiling, twisted fabric
The coiling fabric.

Illusion of the plant,
illusion of the atom and galaxy.

Unfolding spiral motion.

Shifting through the medium.

Rind/ visual of the field
The rind on all the fruit,

Their skin, and innards
the screen,

the field.

Secrets of the metals.

Secrets of the sun.

Shapes of frequency,

Map of the galaxy.

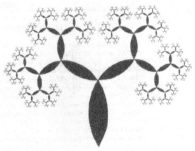

The Screen of Reality
Hexagonal screen pattern.

The fabric before you.

The oscillating magnetic,
electric field.

The web.

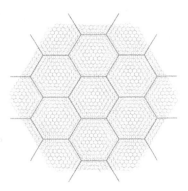

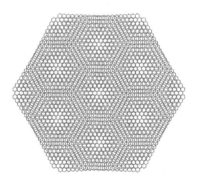

Stretched or Crushed/ the burning web

The body will burn,
or freeze,
where ever it is placed.

Ripped
in the cool, and hot spots of space.

Crushed
burned,

into oscillation of rings.

Sacred geometry.

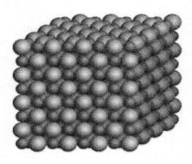

Compression,
expansion
into cubes.

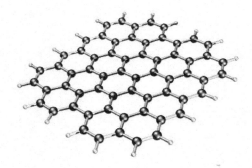

Freezing/ capped column/fruits of the phenomenon

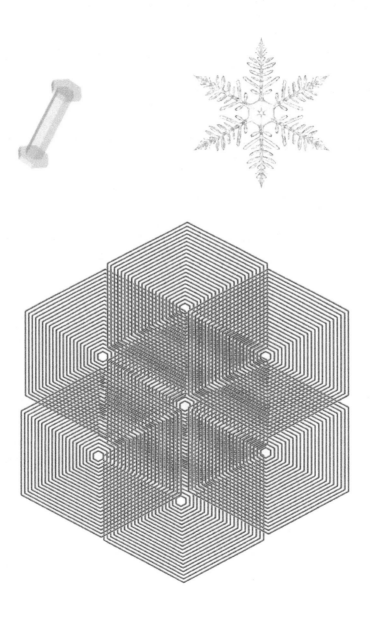

The X and Y of Motion
The sun soaking earths water,

letting it loose in its shadow.

Fog, air, the cloud.
the wind, rain and waves.

Weather.

The x and y motions.

The Inverse of the Universe
I stand over all the gorgeous, bright galaxies.

Like a giant,
stomping on all the pretty colours.

Parent of motion.

I wear the universe;

My outer skin.

The X and Y of existence.

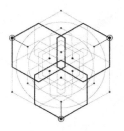

The inverse of the universe.

The original sin.

Philosophy/ phi
The divine proportion

Unification.

The one, the all.

The art of motion.

Law that governs the universe.

Shapes of the fabric.

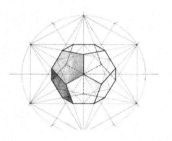

The root of reality.

The knowledge of everything.

Geometry of man;

God,
and thy love for wisdom.

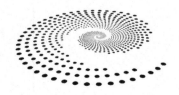

Truth of the Matter/ poetry and magnetism
I will leave you with the dark,
enlightening truth.

It is you.

The one.

God of the earth.

It,
motion,
and that,
mind.

Poetry,
magnetism.

That which is;

Laughter.

Thy reflection.

The breath,
and joke of consciousness.

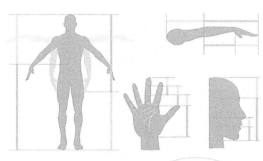
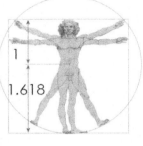

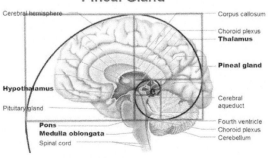

Made in the USA
Columbia, SC
03 June 2024

36211974R00088